Iran Memories and Other Poems:

an Iranian-American Woman's Journey

Zahra Karimipour

ISBN: 978-1-4669-7484-5 (sc)
ISBN: 978-1-4669-7486-9 (hc)
ISBN: 978-1-4669-7485-2 (e)

Library of Congress Control Number: 2012924333

Trafford rev. 02/14/2013

www.trafford.com

North America & international
toll-free: 1 888 232 4444 (USA & Canada)
phone: 250 383 6864 ♦ fax: 812 355 4082

Contents

Acknowledgements

I express my gratitude to the English department at Oklahoma City University for selecting my poetry for publication in the university's literary journal *The Scarab*. I also offer my gratitude to the humanities division of Rose State College for selecting my poetry for publication in the college's literary journal, *Pegasus*.

I thank my husband, friends, and colleagues who read my poetry and encouraged me to publish it.

This book is dedicated to my late mother

Keshvar

And my brothers

Houshang and Akbar

Who raised me lovingly, sacrificed immensely,
and gave me roots

Part One

BORUJERD, THE VIBRANT

Long Gone, But Living

Down that long, narrow alley
Sits an old house of mud brick
With large wooden doors, so aged and rough
As if they are ancient
Heavy, squeaky, they dwarf and engulf me

My small hands press on the giant doors
And I alight into the courtyard
Two giant poplars grow like arms
Two arched, low rooms make the eyes on right and left
Bright pink periwinkles adorn the high walls to the right
But at their feet
Sits the cave-like, dark, monstrous room

Bread is baking here
Large heads of beets and pumpkins are in the cave's belly
To transform into food fit for the gods
The aroma fills me, intoxicates me, makes me impatient

I sprinkle the courtyard with water
And take in the scent of brick
It is early October
Tea Boils on the majestic *Samovar* set on the large wooden cot
On which lies the threadbare, red Persian rug
Waiting to be filled with people of Olympus, in my childhood eyes

Mother and neighbors join
Talking, laughing, drinking tea, tasting the Manna
Creating the heavenly sight
They are, perhaps, oblivious to

I look at the scene awe-struck
Sounds, scents, tales, and memories
All invite me to become part of my childhood home

But only in my dreams
Only in my dreams!

2005

Borujerd's* Winter Night

Night's black veil is on my town
It's a winter night
Streetlights cast hazy shadows
On the old, bent man walking home
On the mother and child, ghostly shadows
Rushing home to flee the cold winter night

A man old, cold, and silent
Is waiting, out in his chariot seat
Looking tiredly, to be told a destination
So he may go on that cold, harsh winter night

Woman and man mount, like kings and queens of the movies
Helping their young in
To watch the horses lap the streets
Cold horses, tired horses, they seem to be

Children's laughter fills the air
They are riding on the winged horses, it seems

The ragged man smiles
Lightly whips the horses
And whispers songs from his steaming mouth
In the harsh, cold winter night

The horses' hoofs are loud
Ta ta . . . ta ta . . . ta ta . . .
The only sounds in the silence of the cold winter night

"Boro yalla, boro yalla," mumbles the charioteer
His mouth sending vapor into the air
His frozen hands dry and callous
Swinging the whiplash, to command and reign
In the harsh, cold winter night

Ragged-layered and wrinkled
Is this lonely figure of the night
Cold, numb and toothless
Out on the chariot
Driving men, women, and children
In the harsh, cold winter nights

These agents of the night
Are the spirit of the town
Leading horses day and night
All seasons
And in the harsh, cold winter nights

Silent and pensive, they are the soul of my town
Always serving, they are the heart of my town

2006

* Borujerd is a small town, west of Iran, in Lorestan Province

6

Mehregan Elementary

Still remember the air that made our noses to glow red
Walking to school in black, shiny boots
Immersed in water and mud, lovingly caressing the rain

Still remember the cold
Hid our heads in our bosoms tight
To walk that long way in our little girlish might

Also remember the sun
Walking on dry autumn leaves
"Crunch," "crunch," "crunch," and "crunch"
Music to our wondering ears

Mehregan got near soon
Stepped into the threshold firm
Felt like the moon amid the stars

Ran, giggled, made circles with other girls
Showed off ribbons, shoes, and pin
Told tales of notebook and pen
Girlish voices ringing loud, just like sounds of *parias**

Umbrella of shiny hairs
We then sat us down again until . . .

Ding, ding, ding, ding, ding, ding, ding . . .
Rang the bell, and each class lined up in a tail
First grade, second grade
Third, fourth, fifth, and sixth grade, all girls
For the morning process, all ears

Then the principal Ms. Hemati said
This girl and that, that girl and this come to the center of the yard
Since you're exemplary in every way
"I've checked their outfits and finger nails," said she aloud
"Everyone be neat and tidy like them school wide"

Then there came hot milk in steel cups for all
To be had with sugar cubes white
Right there in the chilly yard

Still taste that milk today
As I warm up my milk just like that every day

Classes marched softly to the rooms
And we all sat at our wooden benches one by one
The heater flamed dragon-like
As gathered three or four of us around
To warm our little hands and feet one by one

As the lady teacher arrived, we all stood up
In awe of that goddess bright

She checked everyone as she walked
If she saw an untidy soul
Made sure she told her to clean up

Our day filled with lessons, tales, giggles, and fun
Till time came for sweet home and embrace of mom
In blue uniforms and ribbons white
Girls flooded out happy and proud
To walk on dry, cold leaves again
To make them "crunch," "crunch," and "crunch"

2012

Parias are heavenly beings

Childhood Fun

Imagine you in your little town
Fifty or sixty years past
In a narrow alley full of boys, full of girls
In a summer afternoon or early fall
What games you played to keep alive?

We might have had a plastic car
Or a hand-made ugly doll
But never regretted such a lack
Since we played deeply for some fun

No Atari or video games
No TV, video, or VCR
No sophisticated Batman, Superman
Or Barbie dolls

How in the world we got along
In that narrow alley all summer long
Hamid, Saeed, Shahab, Mahmood, Majid
Azam, Pari, Shahin, Mahin, Mehry, Shahnaz
Gathered round with rocks in hand
Which didn't cost any at all

They sat themselves down on the ground
Carried rocks on back of hands
And some they put on the ground
Bet how many could throw in the air
And how many they could catch
While collecting from the ground
"Ye Ghol De Ghol" was the game
They played, laughed, won, and lost
Bet that was lots of hearty deal and talk
When eyes met and veins bulged
To prove that they honestly scored
This was real work and deal
Not staring at a dumb computer screen

Another game, favorite of all
Was turning wheel of a broken bike
And push it down the alley with a stick
On and on
Girls and boys waited their turns
To be the wheel's master for one, two, or three rounds
Oh, Golly was this fun!
Made the wheel run as long as it spun
What better exercise than this?
Hearts and lungs and muscles all
Took part in that Olympic run
This was real work and deal
Not staring at a dumb computer screen

How about those other games?
Dodge ball, Badminton, or Hopscotch
Or bike renting in the neighborhood or school yard
As far as we can know, we were engaged in active fun
Throwing, catching, getting bulging veins
To prove we honestly scored
This was real work and deal
Not staring at a dumb computer screen

Childhood obesity?
No doubt" NO"
Childhood boredom? Not that we could see
Rivalry for better toys? Not that we could perceive

Parents were lucky those days too
They had the wisdom and the truth
Too many toys spoiled children's joy
So content we were, our parents too
Turned out as normal as we could do

Then at night
As soon as we had something light
We were deep in sleep tight
Running, breathing outdoor air
Smelling roses in the yard
Taught us things of land and air
Plus plenty of oxygen
Other attributes were rosy cheeks
With no fat or double chins

2012

Bread Sellers

Carriage wheels' musical sounds
Pedestrians' footsteps, tapping sounds
Everyone lively, agile and fast
Straight, crosswise, come and go
Bumping into other passers-by
Dance on stage one can surmise!

Midmorning air crisp and soft
Men and women purchasing goods
Children to their mothers hang
Cry one minute, the other laugh
Shrills plentiful fill the air
Day has begun. Spring life for sure is on

"Nooneh dugha,"* "Bado Biya,"*
"Bado Biya," "Nooneh dugha," rings aloud
Bread sellers yell their goods
Line the street, squatting like umbrellas
One here, one there, many they are
As far as eyes can see

Dolls in stores' windows they are
Of every *"Lori"* * dress style
Blouses of crimson red and blue
Of lilac, orange, and maroon
Black, beaded vests over blouse
Headbands adorned with nickel coins
Jingle while their heads they turn

Of shapely bodies these women are
Rock-like faces these women have
Faces tinted by the sun, their eyes with vigor shine
Silky luminous their hair is
Brownish are their cheeks and hands
With tough labor touched they are
Majestic with youth are the young
The old traced are by time
With no care, seemingly all of them are

Get close and ask for some bread
They laughingly hand you what they made

Moon's face is their fancy bread
Round, thin, tender, of mythical grade
Rolled on the hot, round stone in the wild
By dandelions, ponies, and their tent
Facing mountains, by streams
Streams their spirit is
Land and sky their comrades, their ease

Free are these men, women
Bear their kind, raise their kind
Under the sun
In the earth's lonely embrace

A few" rials"* their tantalizing bread
Made on the round, smooth, black stone on the rocks
Under the bluest sky
By their tent, their horse, goat, and child
Beside desert thorns, flowers wild

Streets of Borujerd
Breathe with these women's sight
They rest on Borujerd to sell their edible art
They are the heartbeats of my town
In my childhood eyes

2012

* "Nooneh dugha" = bread right out of the oven
* "Bado Biya "=hurry up and get over here!
* Lori= adjective, belonging to Lorestan province
* Rials=unit of money in coins. 100 rials=1 toman bank note

The Woman of "Lorestan"*

You sit on the ground
Under you lying the threadbare, aged Lorestani* rug
Alive in orange red, in paisleys of darkened
Green and blue
Manifesting the gravels underneath
It is no soft surface

The wall of the room you face
It is an old wall, a cracked wall
Manifesting the damp for years at the root

The wall shows years in turquoise blue
Like the walls in Taos Pueblos* homes
An alcove plastered on the wall, holding an old oil lamp
The sole ornament of your rugged, yet lively dwelling

You sit on the ground
Your skirt, an umbrella of
Blue, orange, yellow, and green, a tenacious sphere
Your vest is of black taffeta worn on
The tight red blouse with pale ruffles
On which falls your translucent pink headscarf tightened at
    your young chin

You are the power of Lorestan!
With firm brownish skin as soft as your horse's fur
Shining, strong eyes, strong brows, lips
And hands

And your loom stands tall upon which your hand moves
Like those of Orpheus'* at the harp
To weave colored dreams unto the rug

You are a weaver
In silence weaving magic
Are these magnificent
Hues and shapes
The tongue of your soul, impregnating with life
My bare floors

Are you Athena,* the adroit weaver
Whom no others could rival?
Has your loom become your voice?
Are you speaking your life story in the threads
Walked on heedlessly?

Are you the divine Penelope*? Does your tapestry
Weave magic to restore faith?

You sit for hours on end
To weave destiny
Your immortal tale
To adorn countless homes
Aware or immersed in oblivion
Of what your toil truly is

Yet in the blue and mauve hues of my rug
I see your strong hands, Orpheus-like
Little by little
Weaving colorful threads into the designs
Reminding me incessantly of your days and nights
At the loom
And the child turning inside of you
Destined to become a weaver like you

2008

* *Lorestan* is a province located in west of Iran
* *Lorestani*= belonging to *Lorestan*

This poem reminisces about the time my family and I visited the villages "Donga Serenja" near Borujerd. This weaver stands in my memory in her colorful, humble home, but in her intense artistic moments.

* Taos Pueblos=ancient Native American village, 1000 years old, near Santa Fe, New Mexico
* Orpheus= musician and poet in Ancient Greek myth
* Athena=goddess of wisdom, warfare, and handicrafts in Ancient Greek myth
* Penelope= Odysseus' wife in the ancient Greece epic The Odyssey, composed by Homer

Yalda* Night

Hard to forget that sphere* of warmth
Where our whole bodies went on winter days
Silver flakes we lovingly watched to make huge mounds by the door
But we had no care in the world, just watched them gracefully fall

Mother was coming and going all day long
Preparing a feast of nuts, all kinds
Walnuts, almonds, and pumpkin seeds
Peanuts, cashews, hazelnuts
She put in an antique silver dish
Enough for an army of relatives

She then cut open pomegranates divine
Set a large plate of these pearls aside
Persimmons orange bright and soft
Towered a bowl these tasteful fruits of paradise

19

Orange, grapefruit, and tangerine
Adorned an old tray of hand-made silver of Isfahan*
Grapes red, green, and black
She placed round cuts of water melon red bright

She set oily *Baghlavas** round a tray of gold
The middle she filled with other sweets bold
Our home was a treasure trove of goodies now
Which we didn't dare to touch
Until it was nine at night when uncles, aunts, and guests
     will arrive

Guests surrounded the *Korsi*,* the warm delight
And some sat round the monstrous heat
Joyous, jolly, with frozen feet
Guests came on foot in the deep snow
This was the custom of days gone by

No complaint of snow and cold
They came laughingly and proud
This was their country's special night
Yalda, the ancient festival
They observed in that winter night

One took a "zarb"* and one a "daf"*
The sound of music began the night
So men and women danced around
As we children stealthily ate
Of the fruit and nut all we want

Then announced the elder of the night
"It was time for Hafez 'Faal"*
He asked all to make a wish
So he'll read from Hafez to answer the wish
Murmurs of delight came to faces of all
As he opened the book to begin another *faal*

The History of Yalda Night
A relative of age and stature told us then
"This is the longest night of year
When seeds were gathered, planting done
Ancestors gathered to give their thanks
For a good year of crops and birth of sun"

"Birthday of *Mitra*,* birthday of sun
We're welcoming longer days, shorter nights
As we approach three winter months"
"Teach your youngs to celebrate Yalda Night
To keep our old tradition of *cheleh** alive"

As he sat down to eat, music again sounded sweet
They all drank tea and ale, to keep the memory alive and well

In every home on December 21, Yalda will step far and wide
Tis the Persian Thanksgiving
Ancestors ancient observed of old
To welcome winter and the sun

2012

* Yalda means birth, the birth of light to triumph over darkness
  with passage of autumn
* Sphere of warmth= this metaphor refers to *Korsi*. A *korsi* is a
  square, wooden table-like structure under which a tray of lit
  coals was placed and on top of it a heavy, cotton comforter
  was spread. On each angle of *Korsi* a mattress was laid out for
  household members to enjoy the warmth underneath, while
  the comforter covered their legs and upper extremities. In
  later years, the tray of coal was replaced with a heat lamp,
  which was not quite the same as the coal tray. *Korsi* was kept
  warm all day and night in winter.
* *Isfahan*= Iran's third largest city, south of Tehran

21

* *Baghlavas*= middle-eastern sweets made with oil, flour, sugar, and pistachios
* *Zarb and daf*=musical instruments
* *Hafez Faal*= a reading from the renowned Persian poet Hafez to correspond with the audience's wish
* *Mitra*, an ancient divinity, mentioned in Zoroastrian Avesta, which means "*Mehr*," synonymous with friendship and love. Iranians renew their wows with family during this night
* *Cheleh*=another commonly-used term for *Yalda*

Part Two

IRAN, THE BEAUTIFUL—
1970S

Oh, Caspian!

Oh, Caspian!*
Uproot me
Take me, float me, set me in your tides
Lift me, lower me, raise me
And cradle me onto your shores

Let me grow by you
So with every zephyr
I will stretch my arms and breathe your air
To nourish my fragmented soul

Let me grow by your infinite breast
So my roots will spread far and wide
To house in your soft sand
To be mesmerized once and for all

Let me grow by your sacred, ancient body
So I may hold a nest
On which will fall the rays of your setting sun
The hues of your magnificent rainbow

Let me grow by your greatness
So your rain will absolve me
Your snow will purify me
To become whole again
Like years past when I left you

If you take me in
I will proclaim myself
The Phoenix
Reborn, re-grown, relived
A lesson to all
For ages to come

2005

* The Caspian Sea lies north of Iran

The Old Tehran Is No More

Ah, Tehran!
Show us your majestic face again
Your prolific gardens of violets and roses
Surrounding your serene courtyard pond
That made dwellings paradise-like

Summer time refuge of our little hands and feet
The pond surrounded with myrtle and morning glory
Showed our images in ripples, distorted our noses and lips
Sources of childhood laughter

The courtyard is no more
The pond is long gone
Myrtle and morning glory are not climbing the neighbor's walls

Now the cement, factory-like floor
Houses the modern speaking elevator
That takes us to the floors as high as Alborz Mount
No glossy pond, no velvety flowerbeds
No water-splashed courtyard in summertime
Where we girls picked pink periwinkles to patch our lips in color

Nature is in hiding
Surrounded by walls and windows are children from whom
    the sky hides
Curtains veil the windows into obscurity
Mask the sun, the wind, the cloud
Create the box-like destiny
Into which babies are born and grown

Ah, Tehran!
Yearning for your pure face once more
Show us what you used to be
Vast, restful, and free
Where nature offered repose
And heartbeats grew calm in the presence of a neighbor or two
Where stories were told and souls were restored

Ah, Tehran!
Your modernity has our city in its grips
Smoke, smug, cars, and high-rises are masking your
    cloudless skies
Our skin is scorched. We thirst for rain, but rain is no more
Let your clouds unveil and wash our city clean once more
Let your ancient power restore our city
To the garden of paradise it used to be
Bring to life the apple tree, the quince tree, violets and roses
That embraced the glossy pond
Where our images laughed and our little fingers made ripples

2008

Nowruz

Wheelbarrows of hyacinths, purple and pink
Bowls of gold fish, parsley, myrtle, sprouts of wheat
Nuts of every kind, towering wheelbarrows
Confectionaries in luxurious shop windows
Fragrance in the air

Colored lights, festive thresholds
Fashions and colors, shops adorned
All a grand scene to behold

Energy affluent in passers-by
Faces glowed
Eyes searching, complexions rich, moods jovial
The sight and scent of all claim "Nowruz will soon come"

Streets Restless with men and women
Filling their bags with goodies, their hearts with hope
Rushing toward buses, taxi cabs
Or car keys in hands
Take the goodies home to celebrate the arrival grand

Glorious *Sofreh** of *Haft seen** spread in every home
Seven items shine on termeh* cloth of silver and gold
*Sabzeh,** *Seer,** *serkeh,** *somagh,** *sekeh,** *seeb,** *senjed**
Candlesticks grand, a mirror and coins
Hyacinth, painted eggs, herbs
All placed tastefully on
To bring the news of fertile Farvardeen*
Pregnant with Spring, Nowruz, the Persian New Year!

Homes open to family, to friends
Who come in new clothes, to gather round
To feast, to forget the grievances of the year gone by
Elders giving kids paper money for good omen
Kids jumping with joy, glowing eyes, pounding hearts

Haft S*een*'s glory, world's rejuvenation, all boast
But the words of *Shahnameh,**they revere most
The Great Ferdowsi* composed in thirty years his epic
To give Persians their identity meek
Revived the Persian tongue, with his wise words of the old
Parsi* remained despite attacks of Arabs' force

This is Persia or Iran in spring
Keeping alive Nowruz
Of thousands years past
Persia's Father to us bequeathed

Achaemenid Empire's first King
The World-Renowned, the Tolerant, the Liberator
Cyrus the Great!

2012

* Sofreh= table cloth
* Haft-seen= seven items which symbolize growth, newness, and rebirth of nature.
* Sabzeh, wheat or lentils sprouts= fertility, renewal, growth
* Seer, garlic= medicine; health
* Serkeh, vinegar=renewal
* Somagh or sumac= energy
* Sekeh, coins=prosperity
* Seeb, apple=health
* Senjed, the dried fruit of the oleaster tree= love
* Farfardeen= the first month of spring which starts on March 20 or 21.
* Parsi is the correct name of the Persian language, commonly pronounced "Farsi," which is the Arabic pronunciation.

Part Three

I AM HOME

Mother

At a time when some planned their daughters'
Young marriages
With old men, wealthy men
Reputable men of the town
Mother looked away from the thought

At a time when marriage seemed a way to fortune for girls
Mother championed the classroom
Teachers, paper, pen, and books

At a time when university for girls was not the norm for some
Mother hungered for mine
She was for knowledge free of prejudice
For neglecting the time's stigma
Limitations

At a time when obedience to limiting laws seemed the norm
She taught me to look away
To not fall in the trap of public opinion
The demands of empty social rules

"Liberty is education"
"Independence is education," she often claimed

Free thinking and insightful
She encouraged stepping forward
Being bold to see the truth
Yet doing what was just
She applauded diligence, fairness, compassion
She believed "head" and "heart" must combine

Yet mother could not read or write
Had been married off for wealth and name
Thus knew she had been deprived
But richly educated in the ways of the world
Looked beyond her time
Saw for women a free horizon
Despite the odds

Mother, an Iranian woman
Defied the stereotype
Made freedom "ring"*
She was my Rosa Parks*
Who tore the burdens of the time
So I could roam in the garden of life
Free to think, free to choose, free to be . . . .

2008

* "Let freedom ring" in Dr. Martin Luther King, Jr.'s speech
   "I Have a Dream"
* Rosa Parks=an African-American civil rights activist

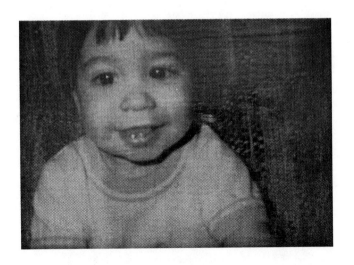

A Little child at Play

Round-eyed and curl-lipped
Rosy-cheeked and curious
The child searches for meaning out of things

She seizes, squeezes
Checks, smells, and tastes things she grips

With numerous touches, plenty of giggles
With thousand questions and many more gestures
The child searches for meaning out of things

Searching, touching, asking, and learning
The little angel continues to grow

1996

Empty Nest

My sons
This week in remembrance of your days at home
We are planting two pear trees
Our yard—undergone preparation—
Already has become significant

The pear trees
Will remind us of your fun spirits
Of what you said and what you did
Of your playful presence at home

Of your jovial souls
Of livelihood, of loving life
Of your curiosity, your wit
Your words, your traces, your notes
Your kindness and treats
Of your playful presence at home

The pear trees
Will make our empty nest full with your memories
Watching them grow
May fulfill our longing
So we may crave you less
To tolerate your absence
A bit easier

2004

Handle with Care

Life is delicate, like a spider's silken web
Like the petals of a rose
Easy to fall at the touch
Sure to break, pulled or exerted

Life is like a seed planted for fruit
Which sun and rain will thrive
Care of the mind, of heart, of soul
Will grow life rich
Left unattended, it will wither and dry

Life is like a fragile vase
May fall and shatter, if shaken hard
Should be pampered
Carefully, wisely
Left ignored, it will lose its bond

Life must be perceived as the universal soul
Examined often to nourish right
Enrich with music, books, and art
Refresh with gentle minds
Whose circle our comfort, security, and delight

2007

Who Is That Woman?

Who is that woman?
Harder than the Alps?
More infinite than the Pacific, or the Red Sea?

A rock?
Which stands the "test of time?"

Or a nest rebuilt on and on
Destroyed by a hand
Which finds her grown at the wrong spot?

A rainbow of magnificent hues
Which fall on ignorant walls?

Is she rain to moisten the soul of the greens?
Music to dispatch cold and grief
Who is that woman?

A dancer dancing to the whim of the weak?
Waiting to rise freely with the wind?

A singer unheard?
The silence of a dark soul?
The tool of a bruised life?

Who is that woman?
She is a hyacinth—waiting for spring to arrive

2004

This Tree Is You and I

It is December
As I walk my morning route
The cold pierces my eyelids, stings my eyes
But I peer at the world
Wondering how nature undefended bears the cold

Standing majestically
Are these heralds of nature
Tall tress, small trees, bare trees
Bare to the bone

These trees are you and I
And we all, I marvel

If you, the passenger of this unpredictable journey
Have a moment to take notice
Stay and gaze
Gaze at the bare bodies
And wonder at the life beneath

Put your hands in the soil
And dig deep. Dig deeper
Until you touch a root
There you find lying
All the reasons to make the tree
Tall, strong, resisting the coldest of the cold

The sun, the rain, the heat, the cold
All have united to penetrate the soil, to shape
What stands majestically robust

These trees are you and I
Our stories, too, lie in our bones
And in our very veins where blood runs
Here are the roots that have shaped us
Words, touches, praises, or blames
Have penetrated our bloods

To make us who we are today
Facing the world
Shaking at the slightest wind
Or standing up tall to thrive

2007

The Brave Crow*

Crow on hot asphalt
Oh, golly, barefoot is
Will it get blisters?

2012

• A haiku for Oklahoma summers

"A traditional Japanese haiku is a three-line poem with seventeen syllables, written in a 5/7/5 syllable count. Often focusing on images from nature, haiku emphasizes simplicity, intensity, and directness of expression" (www.Poets.org)

Freedom Imagined

One day in a train station on a bench
Sitting by me was a dejected soul
This woman murmured these words:

"The caged bird that flies away
Tastes freedom on the horizon
Seeing scenes, highs and lows
Breathing air
Wind lifting it to flight
Mixing with clouds
Refreshing every pore of its flesh"

Why so surrendered? Said I
And heard

"Want to be that bird to fly high
To leave my rotten existence to the wind
To indulge in uplifting pleasures of the soul
To read great works, discuss ideas, art
A future in which the mind does matter
And prejudice, ignorance, and bigotry die"

2002

Days of our lives

Days of our lives are colored
Color is the awakening with the sound of autumn wind
The crisp, cool morning air in your cheeks
Forehead caressed by the morning dew

Color is sitting by the window to sip your morning coffee
To watch the leaves fall one by one
At the foot of the tree
To tiptoe, rustling in the morning sun
Color is hearing the footsteps of the leaves

Color is autumn's reddish hue
The yellow leaves beneath your feet
Their hissing sound in the wind
Flowing like a stream

Color is the lethargic afternoon
Filling you with words and thoughts
Of an era past in the navel of history and time
To unite you with those
Now ghostly shadows in your mind

Color is the magical night
As quiet as the cave in the belly of wilderness
Which hides from all, and you
Drowned in thoughts of a day gone by
And the next soon to come

Color of life
Is the universal pulse
At the rich and the poor's disposal
Throbs in those who perceive its sights and songs
For the next day color to come along

2012

New York City

New York City
Your grandeur many count
And many ask which other city is like you?

You're a symphony of sights
Rows and rows of shops make you so
Leaving no space in between
Book shops, restaurants, souvenir shops, flower shops
Make you a lively city of people on the go

Jewelries, shawls, hats, boots, bags, shoes fill the
    wheelbarrows too
Orange, green, blue, pink, and red are the sights
These trinkets vendors sell, with laughter and delight

Plentiful, lush, heavenly refuge are your parks
For tired souls to repose in shade, by hydrangeas
Birds migrant and resident freely roam, just as people do
Pigeons and squirrels hop about
Children's and adults' spectacles all day long

Your underground is pregnant with souls
Millions ant-like go under and
Appear on
A world is above and one below
Feet walking feel the throbbing flow

You're painted yellow all day and night long
Yellow cabs make you so
Passengers hop on, no delay
So many of them are around

Street vendors, arts, artists selling art
Give you that unique big city feel
By-standers subject of artists' whims
Plastered on side of the street for some time

That brown, Dominican woman, gypsy-like
In long black braids and long brownish skirt
With a black vest on top
Gazes at you, moves her hands on paper sharp
Your portrait in minutes done

That Brazilian man, paintbrush in hand
Keeps you motionless right on the curb
Moves his hands quickly on paper up and down
Your caricature in minutes done

Homes of the renowned your museums are
Van Gogh, Monet, Michelangelo, Matisse
Picasso, Renoir, hundreds more

Indulge on-lookers in centuries past
Of life imagined, life erected of their times
To render history through art

Skyscrapers wall your city to infinite height
Architecture and talent reveal your might
Vivacious grandeur gives you the big city name
The Big Apple, America's heart
Heart of many who made you home

Hudson within you, Lustrous energy in you
Shines amid the city, on which ferries freely float
Paint the grand view
High-rise dwellers gaze on and on

Bridges, of connection of lives
Join this side to that side, build a picturesque scene
Architectural wonders of you
Are beheld in awe

Lifeblood of you, Atlantic on your side
Shines with power and might
Holds you in its bosom tight

Your Crowned Queen
High Tower of Liberty Isle
French Bartholdi sculpted with pride
The Lady in Green, Owner of Liberty Torch
Which other city can match?
Countless lives has she touched
In her unmatched embrace
Countless souls has it given dignity and grace
Millions sing your praise
And ask
Which other city is like you?

2012

Nature, Best Teacher

Give yourself to the calm waves
Let them lull you on
Let the sun sting your skin
Its fire to flame your desire to live

Lend yourself to the breeze
Seek the foliage
Let your eyes swim among the reds, yellows, and violets

Yield yourself to the mountains
Become intoxicated
With the air at the height
With the universe at your feet

Immerse yourself in the memories
When friends took you among them
Sat you down
And drank tea with you
When you and they talked without saying a word
Danced in your hearts

Give yourself to the giggles of children
Let their rosy cheeks and firm spirits
Guide you on

Become mesmerized with the light within
Delight in your strength to empower
Let your talent, heart, and soul mentor you on

2008

Can an Immigrant Be Whole?

Can an immigrant be whole
In a far-away land
Far from heart, from city, from soul
Wrapped memories left in the chest of time
With ones to form anew?

Can an immigrant be whole
In a sea of troubles alone
To disentangle adversity
Without the backbone of family love?

Can an immigrant be whole
Missing the growing ups
Births, marriages, farewells,
The essences of being, the flavors of living?

Can an immigrant be whole
Wrapped in the webs of self
Unaware of kins' pain, and joys
Unable to immerse in lives
To feel alive, a part of those to whom she belongs?

Can an immigrant be whole
Not to have taken a brother's hand
Or not listened to the mother's sobs
To comfort, to change a dark world for one
Not to have laughed
With few in a circle who were her
Breath, her blood, her pulse?

Can an immigrant be whole
Without home's mountain air
The valley's green, the village cottage of an old kin
Away from rivers, seas
Sounds of waves forever
Set in the music of her soul?

An immigrant may never be whole
The carrier of a hole in the heart
For those whom he left behind
For a people
City, village, town,
Her cradle, glory
For the trees, her towers
For the home her haven, den of love and hope

She may live in a good world
Yet she often envisions one, all longings and sighs

2012

Alma Mater

Alma Mater!
You summoned me
Some years past
To come and find you
To cross many lands
Many seas
Oceans
To leave my continent, my people, my home

Alma Mater!
You didn't know
This young soul hadn't known separation this vehement
Your summoning knitted a vigorous storm
Frightened of leaving home, yet desirous to find you
A venture not tasted before

Alma Mater!
I was born anew when I met you
Language, customs, gestures
I relearned when I joined you

Alma Mater!
You summoned me to your Red Dirt
And I pitched my tent where you signaled
I became your tapestry
Which you kept weaving painstakingly

You kept weaving me adroitly
Hour by hour, night and day
So you would complete me
Seemed you've succeeded
Yet this tapestry is rich in some fibers
Poor in others
You tried to make it uniform, whole
An exemplary piece
Yet it could not surrender

I am partly that tapestry, partly the soul you summoned
Still don't know many things
Perplexed and unaware, I trudge and wonder
Why this is so and that is such

Your Red Dirt,* your Grand Prairie
I made home
But I'm half the world I left
And half the world I became
The tapestry of two worlds
To neither completely belong

1992

* Oklahoma's red soil

Silver Skin, Silver Hair

That woman in silver skin, silver hair
Who walks in a plump body with a limp
Is eighty-some years old
Even though time has given her arthritic knees
Even though life tried to bend her some
The power of her spirit is ten-fold

She sings, laughs, cooks, and sews
She just takes the good and forgets most
The power of her spirit is ten-fold

Sit beside her for a while
All you'll hear is laughter and joy
She will talk of this memory and that
With a zest you wouldn't know
She will say words upside down or mix them up

A chest of her words you'll have in no time
She laughs at her own expense just to make you laugh
The power of her spirit is ten-fold

With a pint of vinegar, water, and sugar right
She will sculpt, in no time, a bag of "Aab nabaat"*
Give her fabric a yard or two
A blouse or skirt in an hour she will sew
Machine doesn't make her art, her fingers do
Needles she moves back and forth, fast
Like a machine at a factory, believe it or not
Does she wear glasses at all?
As if born yesterday, her eyes are still sharp
She used to say jokingly,
"God gave me the eyes smallest, the sharpest though!"
"Better use them or else might lose them so"

Walking the streets in mid morning, waving to this
    neighbor and that
My neighbors knew her well too
Even though their tongue she didn't know
She smiled and said "Hi," the only word she knew
I guess my neighbors could tell
In that one word, many happy thoughts were shown
A heart-shaped, purple pincushion with lace around
She hand-sewed and gave each one
As she left with a heavy heart one September day, 1995

The silver-haired, silver-skinned, my mother was
Neighbors missed her when she was gone
She uplifted them with her spirit that glowed

2012

* Aab nabaat=traditional hard candy to be had with hot tea

From Myrtle to Marigold

A butterfly in the sun, hopping joyfully
From daffodil to rose
From myrtle to marigold
Landing on one, tasting the nectar
Hopping on the other
Tasting new nectar
Filled with intoxication, flies away content
Until another day begins, nectar new it tastes

From classroom to classroom, butterfly-like I went
Saw faces new and old
Potpourri of experiences was told

There were the meek, polite faces
That row who sat next to the back wall
Listened and wrote, rewrote and rewrote

After a degree they were, obedient and sharp
Took in directions right
Passed everything with might

That plump girl who had come back to class in years
Composed so beautifully her words
She didn't believe herself

That fellow and that girl who imitated the writers well
Wrote a poem or two themselves
Had them published in *Pegasus**

That young, tall man who never had the chance
To hold paper and books
Now had a time of his life
And couldn't fathom the fact why
So late now?
Was brilliant and wise
Learned like a wound—up doll

That Hispanic girl in the back of class
Who answered all questions right
Now knew she was fit for this
Learned super fast, her confidence piled up

That woman of China, the only foreigner there
Loved learning, spoke gently
Humbly asked us all to sample her food and green tea

The young, tired girl
Chewed gum seriously
Held a pen playfully
Talked with eyes on the opposing wall
Not facing anyone at all

The heavy older man
With disheveled gray hair and a shirt plaid
With blood-shot eyes of construction work
Who knows of how much
Showed effort for a work sublime

The thirty-year-old mechanic
With scanty, shoulder-length hair
Colored tattoos covered his arms and neck
After a day's long, hard work
Listened, and learned
Wrote the best essays he could
Was the superb student I ever met!

That older woman of kind laughter and eyes
Who was after a degree of some sort
But left and didn't come back
Years later, though, saw me in a store
Embraced and said: "Still remember me of old?"

That tall, cheerful girl
A basketball woman, mom of a little boy
Enjoyed learning much, ate the poems word for word
Wrote one herself too
Then heard she drowned of a seizure in her pool
Oh, there . . . was the chair she sat in
Our class became frozen cold with news so sad
We were not the same without her out of hand

Oh, that woman of twenty years past
Who wove a basket fast
Of yellow and green fibers with a bow at the waist
Said: "I have come back in twenty years"
"Have loved learning and being young again"
Her face still I see whenever that basket I see

Then the rowdy bunch
Of sophisticated girls and guys
Who laughed, learned, and were loud
Extremely out-going and polite
Like those never ever had I taught!

And that class in 1994
Who became stories' people
Also disguised this poet and that
Swallowed stories and poems just like that
Gave me a folder with inscription in gold
Bearing the year, class title and name
That memorabilia will always last

And the fellow who wrote me in years yesterday
To say "Thank you" for what he learned he used

Oh, how can I forget the father
Who took notes
For his disabled, twenty-year-old son
The child, most loveable and sharp
With a laughter and learning love
Turned the class into a memory fine
And passed superbly with high marks
An inspiration was he and his father too
Who wouldn't think there are great souls like them around?

And . . . that famous football player who
Used to write and write repeatedly
With tears in eyes shook my hand
Grateful, humble, an empowered man

That Vietnam Veteran who always sat by the door
Made us all laugh since connected learning with more
Got a "kick" out of stories for sure

His wife, he said, was a painter
Walks to class one day with a large painting rolled
"My wife has drawn this for you," while saying a few
kind words
Where is he now, what does he do?

And numerous military women and men
Who had to leave mid way
To finish from far-away or later years
Integrity and discipline was their creed
Brought to good end their incomplete deed

And the seventy-year-old Mary H.
With gray hair and soft, silver skin
Whose class experience she wrote as a journey of sort
In which we went from country to country, coast to coast
To meet men and women of literary mold
Her poem in a frame I still hold

Many more memories of teaching years
I hold in a blue swollen binder
Binder of cards, notes, letters of old
Which I leisurely peruse
And fill with joy as each face speaks a line
Puts me in that classroom once again

If I should go on with my stories of old
This poem will run for pages and pages more
But this should only suffice
From daffodil to rose
From myrtle to marigold
Have I taken in nectar as sweet as gold

The nectars my nourishment have been
My transformation, for sure
The fibers of my being all

2012

* Pegasus= the literary journal of Rose State college in Midwest
City, Oklahoma.